C000193265

THIS IS A CARLTON BOOK

The Dog Logo and Photographs © 2004
Artist International Inc
Text and Design copyright © 2004
Carlton Books Limited

This edition published in 2004 by
Carlton Books Ltd
A Division of the Carlton Publishing Group
20 Mortimer Street
London
W1T 3JW

A CIP catalogue for this book is available
from the British Library.

ISBN 1 84442 696 3

Project Editor: Amie McKee
Art Director: Clare Baggaley
Design: Stuart Smith
Production: Caroline Alberti

Printed and bound in Singapore

THE DOG
Artlist Collection

NAUGHTY **DOGS**

CARLTON
BOOKS

Miniature Pinscher

Miniature Pinscher

Chihuahua

Chihuahua

Chihuahua

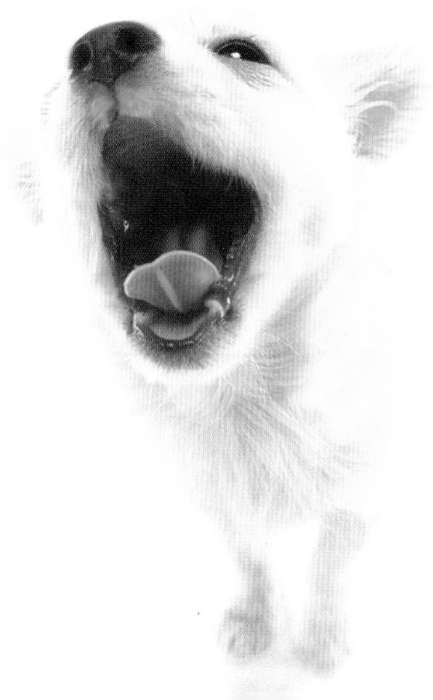

Cavalier King Charles Spaniel

Cavalier King Charles Spaniel

German Shepherd

German Shepherd

Akita

Tosa

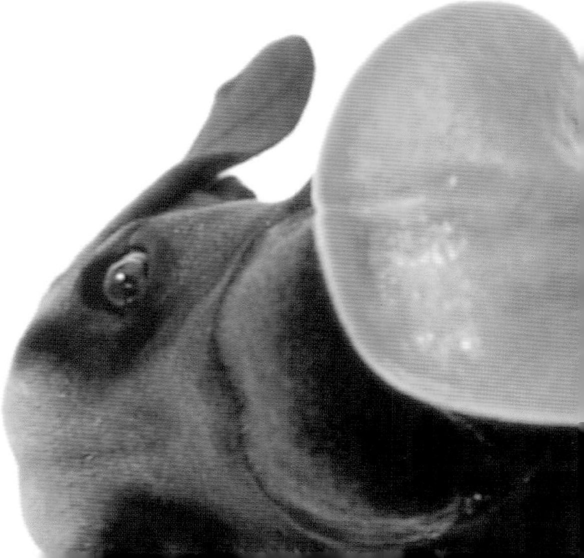

Jack Russell Terrier

Jack Russell Terrier

Labrador Retriever

Labrador Retriever

Manchester Terrier

Siberian Husky

Siberian Husky

Boxer

Boxer

Japanese Terrier

Airedale Terrier

Beagle

Beagle

Beagle

Beagle

Pug

Flat-Coated Retriever

Flat-Coated Retriever

Bernese Mountain Dog

Poodle

Golden Retriever

American Cocker Spaniel

Shetland Sheepdog

Dalmatian

Dalmatian

Pomeranian

Basset Hound

Maltese

French Bulldog

French Bulldog

Miniature Schnauzer

Pembroke Welsh Corgi

Shiba Inu

Dachshund

Doberman

West Highland White Terrier

West Highland White Terrier